# The Good Works Pledge

## by

## Christine Singh

**Second Edition**

Published by

Helping The World LLC

ISBN: 979-8-9955582-1-7

contact@helpingtheworlded.com

# This Book Belongs To

___________________________

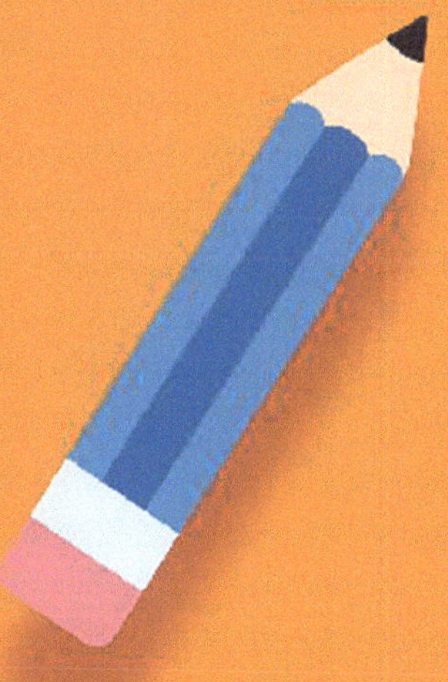

# Table of Contents

Be Kind
Make Someone's Day
1

Be Kind
I will lend a helping hand

# Be Kind
## I will show someone love

# Be Kind

## I will share a smile

# Be Kind

## I will tell someone, "Good day"

# The Kindness Pledge

Let us pledge to be kind to everyone. These special words will help you remember how to show kindness every day.

*Find each word in the puzzle below
and circle it to show you are a kindness champion.*

GOOD DAY   LOVE   KIND   SMILE   HELP

6

# Be Friendly
## Treat someone like a friend

Be Friendly
I will support someone
8

# Be Friendly
## I will share something
## I have with someone who needs it

# Be Friendly
## I will tell someone something I like about them

Be Friendly
I will show someone respect
Let Me Help!
11

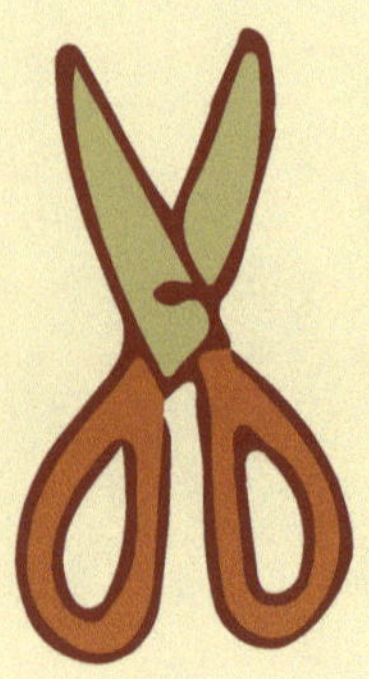

# Write your own friendship promise.

**Think about ways you can be a good friend and write a pledge that tells how you will treat your friends.**

# Be Honest
## Do what is right

13

# Be Honest
## I will tell the truth

# Be Honest
## I will do what is right

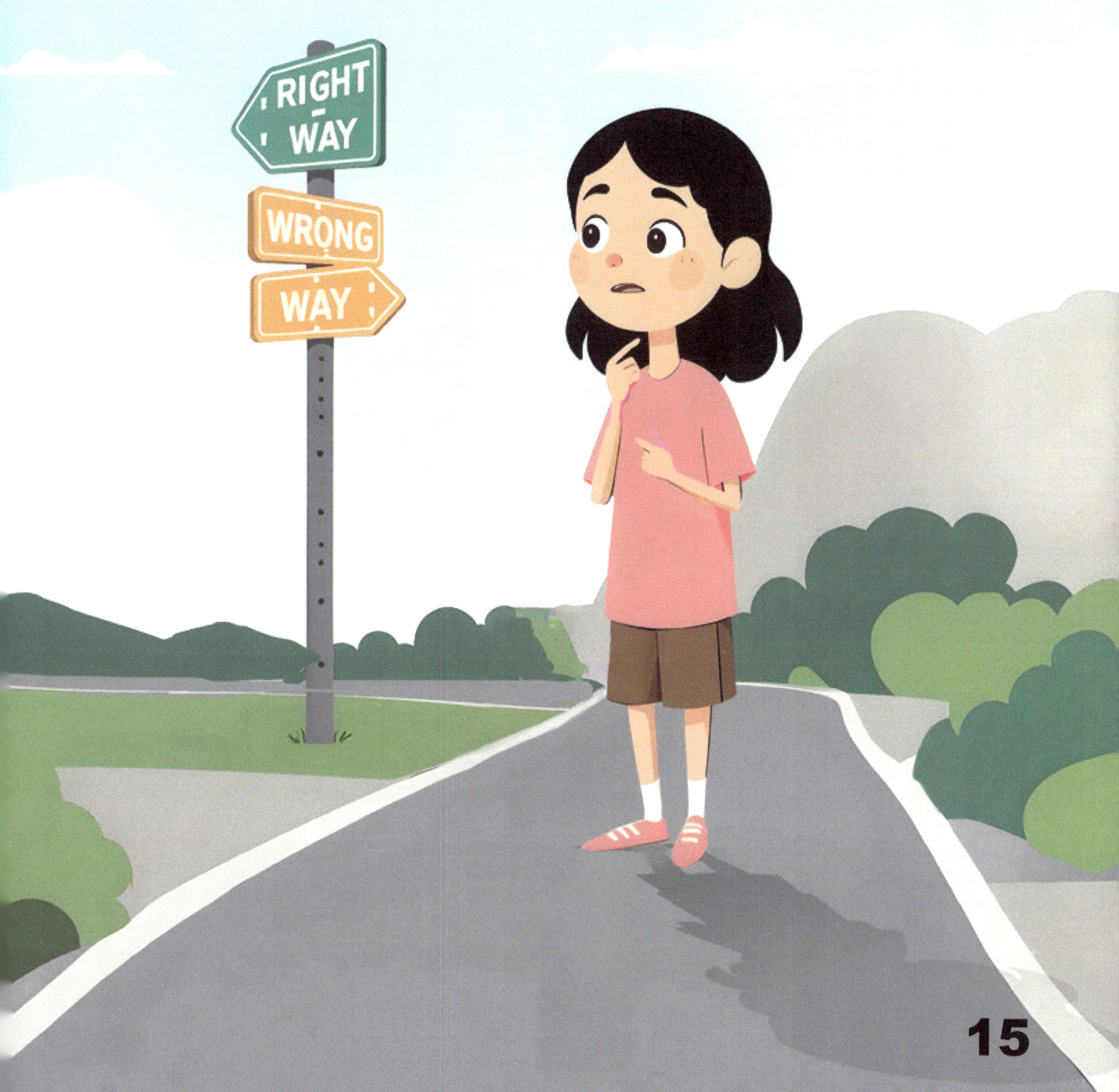

# Be Honest
## I will be fair

# Be Honest

## I will be sincere

# THE HONESTY PLEDGE

Team up with a friend and talk about creating an honesty pledge. Write down one good thing that can happen when you tell the truth, and one not-so-good thing that might happen if you do not.

# Be Determined
## Stick with it

# Be Determined
## I will be strong

# Be Determined
## I will ask for help

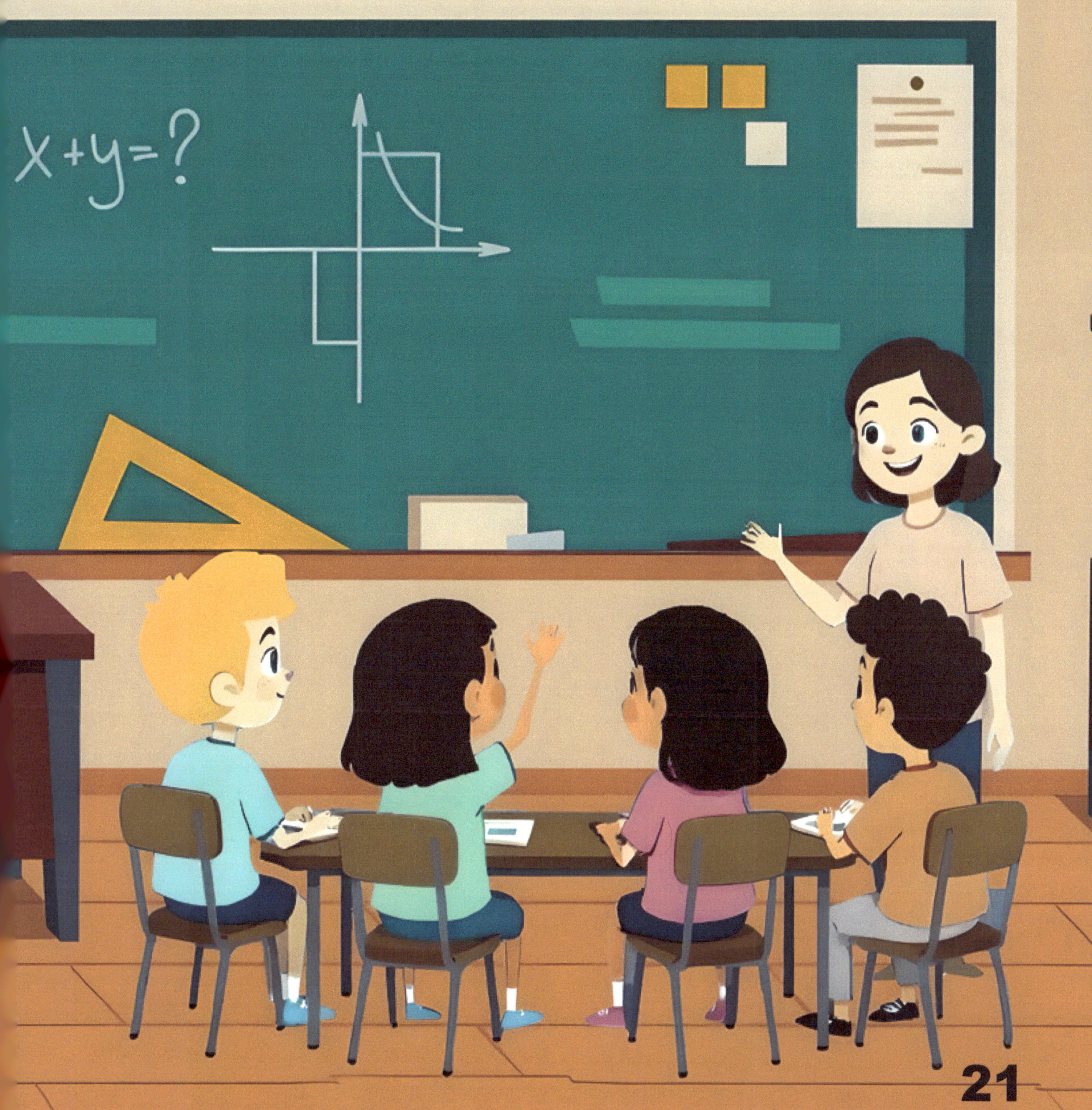

# Be Determined
## I will be brave

# Be Determined
## I will never give up

# THE DETERMINED PLEDGE

Show your bravery and pledge to be courageous.
Draw a picture of a time this week when you did something brave.

# Do Good Works!